FROM PIONEERS TO PRESERVATIONISTS:

A BRIEF HISTORY OF SEQUOIA AND KINGS CANYON NATIONAL PARKS

By Douglas H. Strong

Published by Sequoia Natural History Association

FIRST EDITION 2000

ISBN 1-878441-07-8
Printed in the United States

PUBLISHED BY
THE SEQUOIA NATURAL HISTORY ASSOCIATION

The non-profit Sequoia Natural History Association works in partnership with the National Park Service to provide educational publications and programs for Sequoia and Kings Canyon National Parks and Devils Postpile National Monument. The proceeds from the sale of this book directly benefit these national parks.

For a publications catalog or information on membership, field seminars and other educational programs, call (559) 565-3759 or e-mail: a-seqnha@inreach.com.

Sequoia Natural History Association
HCR 89, Box 10
Three Rivers, CA 93271

Internet web page http://sequoiahistory.org

THANK YOU FOR HELPING SEQUOIA AND
KINGS CANYON NATIONAL PARKS!

FROM PIONEERS
TO PRESERVATIONISTS

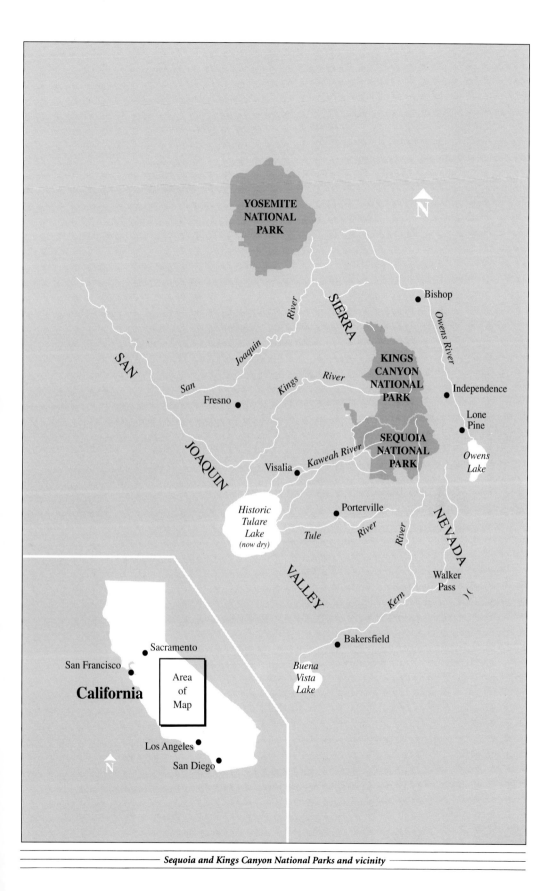

YOSEMITE
NATIONAL
PARK

SIERRA

Bishop

KINGS
CANYON
NATIONAL
PARK

Owens River

Independence

San Joaquin River

Kings River

Fresno

Lone
Pine

SEQUOIA
NATIONAL
PARK

SAN

Owens
Lake

JOAQUIN

Kaweah River

Visalia

Historic
Tulare
Lake
(now dry)

Porterville

Tule River

River

NEVADA

VALLEY

Kern River

Walker
Pass

N

Sacramento

San Francisco

Area
of
Map

Bakersfield

Buena
Vista
Lake

California

Los Angeles

San Diego

N

Sequoia and Kings Canyon National Parks and vicinity

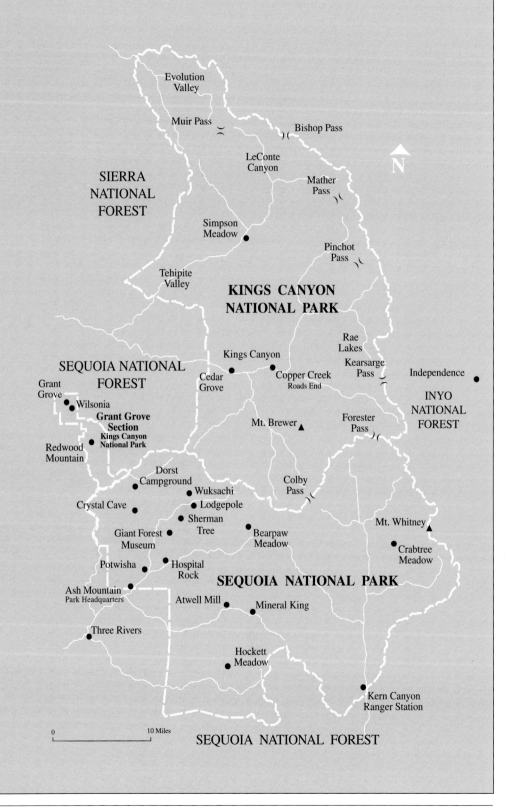

Evolution
Valley

Muir Pass

Bishop Pass

SIERRA
NATIONAL
FOREST

LeConte
Canyon

Mather
Pass

Simpson
Meadow

Pinchot
Pass

Tehipite
Valley

**KINGS CANYON
NATIONAL PARK**

Rae
Lakes

Kearsarge
Pass

Independence

SEQUOIA NATIONAL
FOREST

Kings Canyon

Grant
Grove

Cedar
Grove

Copper Creek
Roads End

INYO
NATIONAL
FOREST

Wilsonia

**Grant Grove
Section**
Kings Canyon
National Park

Mt. Brewer ▲

Forester
Pass

Redwood
Mountain

Dorst
Campground

Colby
Pass

Wuksachi

Crystal Cave

Lodgepole

Sherman
Tree

Mt. Whitney ▲

Giant Forest
Museum

Bearpaw
Meadow

Crabtree
Meadow

Potwisha

Hospital
Rock

SEQUOIA NATIONAL PARK

Ash Mountain
Park Headquarters

Atwell Mill

Mineral King

Three Rivers

Hockett
Meadow

Kern Canyon
Ranger Station

0   10 Miles

SEQUOIA NATIONAL FOREST

N

TABLE
OF
CONTENTS

PREFACE

IN 1950, A FRIEND AND I, TEENAGERS IN SEARCH OF AN ADVENTURE, hoisted our vintage Trapper Nelson backpacks and hiked over Kearsarge Pass into the upper reaches of Kings Canyon National Park. In the days that followed, we rarely encountered another person. Much of the vast wilderness of the High Sierra lay essentially untouched, preserved in Sequoia National Park (1890) and Kings Canyon National Park (1940). Subsequent backpacking trips stimulated my curiosity about the region, and eventually I wrote a booklet, then entitled *Trees—or Timber? The Story of Sequoia and Kings Canyon National Parks* (1968), that focused on the parks' early history.

This completely revised edition brings the story of both parks up-to-date. I am particularly indebted to geographer Lary M. Dilsaver who generously gave me permission to borrow liberally from our co-authored article, "Sequoia and Kings Canyon National Parks: One Hundred Years of Preservation and Resource Management" and to the publication in which it appeared, *California History* (summer 1990). I benefited from *Challenge of the Big Trees: A Resource History of Sequoia and Kings Canyon National Parks*, an informative book coauthored by Dilsaver and historian William C. Tweed. Maps of Sequoia and Kings Canyon are based on those developed from this book. My daughter, Beret E. Strong, provided valuable editorial assistance and suggestions for revisions. I wish to thank the Sequoia Natural History Association for helping plan this booklet and for keeping it available to the public.

INTRODUCTION

GIVEN THE PREVAILING VALUES OF THE SECOND HALF of the nineteenth century, it is a wonder that Congress established any national parks. This was an era of industrialization. Railroad tracks reached westward to an abundance of cheap land made available by a bountiful government. Improved transportation and communication opened markets and encouraged regional specialization. A near absence of regulations gave business enterprise a free hand. Corporations dominated the production and distribution of manufactured goods across the country. Scientific research and development reached a state of organization and success previously unimagined. Thomas Edison's workshop gave way to the mammoth laboratory of the General Electric company, and Henry Ford's assembly line techniques in the early twentieth century allowed for mass production. Technological breakthroughs—the Bessemer process for producing steel, the electric dynamo, the internal-combustion engine—helped transform American life and with it, the American environment.

Unfettered economic growth combined with a belief that the country's resources were inexhaustible resulted in devastation of the land. Loggers denuded forests, hydraulic miners washed away hillsides, hunters decimated wildlife, and stockmen overgrazed grasslands. Not all who laid waste to the land were land raiders, despoilers who saw no reason to use the land with care. Many were honest, hardworking settlers who did not foresee the destructive consequences of their actions. Most simply followed a course of expediency as the best path to success. And as long as the government's land policy was to promote private ownership with the right to use the land as one pleased, it was unlikely that many individuals would practice restraint and good husbandry.

A conservation ethic arose gradually, challenging the wisdom of unchecked utilization of the land. By the time of the Civil War, individuals such as Henry David Thoreau, Frederick Law Olmsted, and George Perkins Marsh recognized the dangers of an expanding population devoted to economic profit. After the Civil War, when private citizens experienced growing shortages of wildlife and forests, they experimented with the propagation of fish and the planting of trees. Congress responded with legislation to encourage such practices. In the 1870s and 1880s, sportsmen's clubs and periodicals proved popular, and citizens' conservation organizations multiplied.

These groups sought to protect natural resources and to provide opportunities for outdoor recreation. They and a handful of others across the land initiated the pleas and protests that helped stimulate a national concern for conservation—for wiser use of resources and for preservation of a few areas of exceptional scenic value.

The first significant step to protect America's scenic heritage came when President Abraham Lincoln signed a bill in 1864 granting Yosemite Valley and the Mariposa Grove of Big Trees to the state of California "for public use, resort, and recreation." While Yosemite was not yet a national park, the national park idea was born when Congress set this land permanently aside for nonutilitarian purposes. Eight years later, Congress created Yellowstone as a "public park or pleasuring-ground for the benefit and enjoyment of the people," the nation's first national park. In 1890, Congress established three more parks—Sequoia, Yosemite, and General Grant—all in California.

Such success did not come easily. The creation of Sequoia resulted primarily from the determined efforts of a few San Joaquin Valley residents who launched a campaign to protect the Sierra watershed and the scenic beauty of some giant sequoias. Expansion of Sequoia and establishment of Kings Canyon National Park came only after extended battles and compromises with a variety of interest groups, including irrigationists and hydroelectric power developers.

Creation of national parks posed one set of problems, their management posed another. The early national parks lacked a common central administration until formation of the National Park Service in 1916. Stephen Mather, its able first director, established guidelines for park management, recruited a corps of trained and dedicated people, and worked to add new areas of outstanding beauty to the park system. He and all those who followed him have had to guard against threats to the parks. The initial danger did not lie so much in the loss of a single valley to a hydroelectric dam and reservoir, or of a mountain forest to a lumber mill, as in the precedent that such a loss would establish. With the passage of time, efforts to meet escalating public demand for campgrounds, lodgings, and other "improvements" resulted in increasing development within the parks. More recently, smog and other pollutants have damaged vegetation and obscured scenic views within many parks.

The story of Sequoia and Kings Canyon National Parks helps illustrate how preservation of scenic lands first took hold in the United States and how management of national parks has evolved over the last century. The efforts of a few individuals saved many of the nation's finest groves of giant sequoias and led to the protection of one of the world's outstanding wilderness regions. The battle to set aside and protect these parks is the prototype for efforts waged for other parks. Let Sequoia and Kings Canyon be lessons in the power of the persistence of the determined preservationist.

1 EARLY EXPLORATION AND NATIVE AMERICANS

WHEN SPANISH EXPLORER JUAN RODRIGUEZ CABRILLO SAILED along the coast of California in 1542, he had no way of knowing that the Sierra Nevada existed. Two hundred and thirty years passed before Captain Pedro Fages and a Franciscan missionary, Fray Juan Crespi, stood at a point near the junction of the San Joaquin and Sacramento rivers and first sighted the high mountains. Four years later in 1776, Franciscan missionaries Pedro Font and Francisco Garcés, members of the first overland party from Mexico, reported "una gran sierra nevada" (a great snowy range) to the east.

Very little resulted from these discoveries. The San Joaquin Valley held minimal interest for the Spanish except as a place to attempt to convert Native Americans to Catholicism, to recapture Native Americans who had escaped from the coastal missions, and to look for stolen cattle and horses. The gold and silver in the mountains lay hidden and the fur-bearing animals attracted little attention in these early years.

While Native Americans knew the Sierra Nevada well, no one of European descent crossed the range until 1827. In that year Jedidiah Smith led a band of Americans across the Great Basin and reached San Gabriel Mission within the territory of Mexico. Although the Mexican governor, suspicious of the interloping Americans, asked Smith to leave the way he came, Smith traveled north into the San Joaquin Valley. Impeded by heavy snow, he finally managed to cross the Sierra, from west to east, in the vicinity of the Stanislaus River and Ebbetts Pass. In 1844, explorer John C. Fremont of the U. S. Topographical Engineers faced similar difficulties, nearly losing his life in a snowstorm in an unsuccessful attempt to cross the range by following the Kings River and its tributaries.

In spite of these visits by Smith, Fremont, and others, the southern Sierra Nevada remained little known. Fur trappers found few beaver in the foothills, and the ruggedness of the mountains discouraged exploration. Not until 1850, shortly after the United States acquired California from Mexico by conquest, did Lieutenant George H. Derby conduct the first official survey of the San Joaquin Valley. His brief report and rudimentary map, however, added little to what was already known of the mountains to the east. Derby, who thought that the Kaweah River drained the entire western slope of the Sierra Nevada, remained totally unaware of the great Kern Canyon.

A second government party, led by Robert B. Williamson, traveled
through the valley in 1853 in search of a railroad route from the lower Colorado River country to the Pacific Ocean. Like his predecessor, Williamson
looked at the Sierra from a distance. In his report he called special attention
to the "Kay-wee-ya" River and to its luxuriant oak-covered delta, whose rich
soil and variety of grasses had already begun to attract American settlers.

Settlement invariably led to exploration of the mountains to the east. In
pursuit of a large party of Native Americans in 1851, Captain John F.
Kuykendall drove a band from its camp on the Kings River toward the
headwaters of the Kaweah, ascending into mountainous country more
rugged than any he had seen before. He and his troops must surely have
seen the Kings Canyon and quite possibly were the first of the newcomers to
view the peaks of the northern section of the future Sequoia National Park.

Native Americans and Hale Tharp

The Native Americans of the Sequoia-Kings Canyon region were
Shoshonean. The Monache (or Western Mono) occupied the lower canyon
country, the Tubatulabal controlled the Kern River drainage area, and the
Owens Valley Paiute (Eastern Mono) dominated the land east of the crest of
the Sierra. All three peoples had contact with one another within the present
area of the parks. A fourth group, the Penutian-speaking Yokuts from the
San Joaquin Valley, also undoubtedly visited the park region from time to
time in order to trade, hunt, and avoid the valley's summer heat. The indig-
enous peoples roamed throughout Sequoia-Kings Canyon country, crossed
the High Sierra passes, and established many of the routes for the mountain
trails used by today's hikers. Obsidian chips beside small lakes attest to
their numerous campsites, while bedrock mortars, used to pulverize nuts and
seeds, are plentiful at village sites in the foothills.

For centuries Owens Valley Paiute had summered in the high mountains
and wintered east of the range. Because of the harsh winters in the high
mountains, some of these people, some 500-600 years ago, established camps
in the western foothills along branches of the Kaweah River and in the lower
canyon of the Kings River. Acorn meal from the abundant oak trees replaced their previous staple of piñon pine nuts, and they maintained an
active trade across Sierra passes with their relatives on the eastern side.
The Paiutes occasionally traveled west as far as the land of the Yokuts,
taking with them such items as pine nuts, obsidian, salt, baskets, and
rabbitskin blankets to exchange for acorns, berries, shell-bead money, baskets, and buckskin.

The Potwisha, a small group of Monache, established the best-known
camp within the boundaries of the future parks at Hospital Rock. This

attractive village site along the Middle Fork of the Kaweah had as its center a huge boulder over a cave that provided a shelter, storehouse, hospital, and summer meeting place. The surrounding region contained a wide variety of plants, animals, and fish. While the Potwisha and other Native Americans of the Sierra foothills lived in relative harmony with the natural environment, their use of fire to encourage new plant growth and to aid in the hunt altered the local vegetation.

Hale Tharp

Soon after the discovery of gold, trouble began between white settlers and Native Americans in Mariposa County, which then included what later became Tulare and Fresno counties. In 1851, the Native Americans of the area ceded their rights to the land between Owens Valley and the Pacific Ocean in exchange for reservations, one of which stretched from the Kaweah River to the Kings and high up into the mountains. The United States Senate, however, rejected this and all other treaties, and the Native Americans' subsequent land claims were disallowed.

Growing numbers of white settlers established homes in the foothills and valleys below. In 1856, Hale D. Tharp left the gold fields near Placerville and settled on the Kaweah River near what later became the town of Three Rivers. Here he found plentiful wildlife and fish as well as grassland to raise cattle. When nearby friendly Potwishas invited him to visit their camps in the mountains, he accepted enthusiastically. Tharp wanted to find a summer range for his livestock and was intrigued by the Native Americans' stories of giant trees. Guided by two young Potwishas, he traveled along the Middle Fork of the Kaweah River to Moro Rock and then to Giant Forest, perhaps the first white person to enter the area. After a few days at Log Meadow, he returned via Hospital Rock.

Two years later, Tharp retraced his steps to Giant Forest and continued somewhere into the Kings River Canyon country. On his return trip some two weeks later, he explored the East Fork of the Kaweah River in the vicinity of Mineral King and returned home by way of Hockett Meadow and the South Fork of the Kaweah. By 1861, he had begun using Log Meadow as a summer range for his horses and he later built a trail to the south end of the meadow for use by his growing herd of cattle.

By this time, others were entering the Three Rivers country. The Potwishas appealed to Tharp to help them protect their land, but there was nothing he could do. Smallpox, scarlet fever, and measles spread from the white population with devastating results. Tharp reported that he personally helped bury twenty-seven people in one day. Native Americans of the Kings Canyon also declined rapidly in number. Some of the survivors retreated into the high mountains and crossed the Sierra into the desert to the east. Others adapted to life on the fringes of rapidly growing white communities in the foothills.

Tharp's Log before restoration

2 EARLY USES OF THE LAND

MOST AMERICANS WHO ENTERED THE MOUNTAINS came for practical reasons: building trails, grazing sheep and cattle, searching for gold and silver, and felling timber. With the discovery of gold in Inyo County, east of the Sierra, in 1859, a virtual stampede of gold seekers crossed the mountains along a route just south of what is now Sequoia National Park. Two enterprising trail builders, John B. Hockett and John Jordan, blazed routes over the mountains after Tulare County supervisors granted them franchises for toll trails. When the Inyo mining boom declined, these ventures failed. Early trails across the rugged mountains could not compete with the longer but much more passable wagon road constructed across Walker Pass to the south.

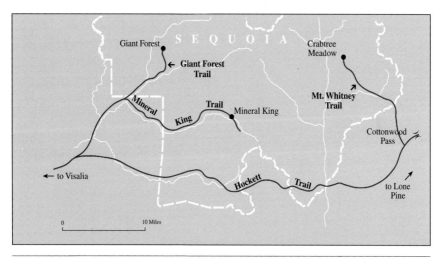

Pioneer trails of Sequoia & Kings Canyon National Parks

Sheepherders made the first important commercial use of the mountains. California, with its mild climate and fertile interior valleys, proved a sheepherder's paradise, but the drought in 1863-1864 compelled herders to search for new grazing land in the coast ranges and the Sierra Nevada. Sheep could range almost to the summits of the highest peaks and proved more adaptable and profitable to own than cattle. While many sheepherders from the southern San Joaquin Valley drove their flocks north and east into the upper Kings and Kern rivers, some herders traveled as far north as Yosemite and Lake Tahoe. Most were French and Spanish Basques

Felling the Mark Twain Tree

Stump of the Mark Twain Tree (stump remains at Big Stump Basin in Kings Canyon)

who received from their American employers a nominal wage, their keep, and a percentage of the increase in the flock. Many local ranchers also drove livestock into the mountains and competed for the available pasture land.

Unfortunately, the era's sheepherding practices, combined with a complete lack of governmental control over the use of public land, resulted in widespread damage to the mountain watersheds. Sheepherders set fires to clear away the brush and deadfall that hindered the movement of their sheep. The routes of the flocks approaching the San Joaquin Valley in the fall could often be traced by the billowing clouds of smoke from fires that ran unchecked over the mountain slopes. When the sheep reentered the mountains as the snow melted each spring, their sharp hoofs cut deeply into the moist soil, severely damaging the meadows.

Prospectors also participated in the exploration and utilization of the Kings, Kaweah and Kern watersheds. These fortune seekers spent years in futile efforts to find mineral wealth until the discovery of silver in 1873 touched off a rush to the high mountain valley of Mineral King. Prospectors eagerly filed mining claims, and the New England Tunnel and Smelting Company (soon renamed the "New England Thieving and Swindling Company") promoted development. Thomas Fowler, a prominent Californian, completed a toll road into the isolated valley in 1879 and built a stamp mill and a tramway to the Empire Mine. These speculative ventures proved unprofitable. The toll road became public but only a few valley residents, attracted by the cool mountain air, continued to visit the valley each year.

Lumbermen had a much greater impact. Logging began soon after the first settlers arrived in the San Joaquin Valley; by the 1860s, several small mills operated on the most accessible fringes of the coniferous forest. Although pine and fir trees provided most of the lumber, many giant sequoias were cut to provide shakes, fence posts, and grape stakes. Some of the finest specimens were cut for exhibition in the east, a practice that began as early as 1853.

The worst was yet to come. Log flumes, introduced in 1889, opened previously inaccessible timberlands to loggers. In 1890, the Kings River Lumber Company began to ship timber via a long flume to Sanger, over fifty miles away. During its operation, this one company (reorganized as the Sanger Lumber Company), felled nearly every tree in the Converse Basin, once the finest stand of giant sequoias in existence.

Converse Basin Mill, just north of Grant Grove

Big Stump, 1888

3 HIGH COUNTRY AND KINGS CANYON EXPLORATION

As LUMBERMEN BEGAN TO ENCROACH ON THE TIMBER BELT,
the California State Geological Survey undertook the first significant exploration of the Sierra, including its high alpine region. Led by William H.
Brewer, a party of five men left for the Kings-Kaweah country in 1864. Early
in June, they climbed a peak from which they could view the whole crest of
the southern Sierra. They named the peak Mount Brewer. For the first time,
the topography of the Kings, Kern and Kaweah watersheds was viewed and
understood by people of European descent. The survey party recognized at
last that the highest crest of the Sierra had been hidden by the peaks at the
headwaters of the Kaweah River and that in between lay the spectacular
upper Kern River Canyon.

Clarence King and Richard Cotter, two members of the party, ventured on
alone toward the highest peaks. They climbed and named Mount Tyndall,
but to their surprise saw two peaks to the south that rose even higher. The
tallest of all they named Mount Whitney in honor of the survey's director,
Professor Josiah Dwight Whitney of Harvard University. While they yearned
to climb to the top of its bold eastern front and snow-trimmed crest, they had
limited food and turned back to rejoin the main party. Further exploration
took the group to Owens Valley and back to the west through the Kings
Canyon, whose grandeur Brewer compared to that of Yosemite. Clarence
King later returned, in two attempts to climb Mount Whitney, only to find
that three Inyo County residents had already made the first ascent on August
18, 1873.

While the Whitney survey identified the major features of the southern
Sierra, much of the backcountry remained isolated. The farthest reaches of
the future Kings Canyon National Park (north of Muir Pass in the watershed
of the San Joaquin River) were essentially unknown until Theodore S.
Solomons explored the area, named the Evolution peaks, and published his
findings in the 1890s. Only then did explorations begin to be detailed and
systematic.

The upper Kern River country also remained little known, especially
since few people left records of their visits. One exception was the Samuel P.
Langely scientific expedition of 1881 that came to study solar radiation on
Mount Whitney. Langely suggested that a shelter be constructed on the
summit for use by future scientific parties. An accompanying map outlined a

proposed military reservation that included the crest of the Sierra from Mount Williamson to Sheep Mountain (Mount Langely) and parts of Owens Valley. President Chester Arthur responded in 1883 with an order to establish the Mount Whitney Military Reservation—apparently to allow the United States Weather Bureau, then under the jurisdiction of the Chief Signal Officer of the War Department, to conduct research. Twenty years later, the War Department relinquished its control; it no longer had jurisdiction over the Weather Bureau and could find no military use for Mount Whitney.

Early park pioneers

4 PRESERVATION EFFORTS AND SEQUOIA NATIONAL PARK

BY THE 1850S, THE SIERRA NEVADA BEGAN TO ATTRACT world-wide attention after a hunter stumbled on the stand of giant sequoias now known as the Calaveras Grove. Together with Yosemite Valley, these enormous trees became meccas for tourists. While the coastal redwoods reached a greater height and the bristlecone pines of California's White Mountains were older, no other species of tree could match the giant sequoia in sheer bulk and grandeur. The largest tree of all (now called the General Sherman) spreads more than thirty-six feet in diameter at its base and stands taller than a twenty-seven-story building. A branch more than six feet in diameter that fell in 1978 would have been a giant among trees on the east coast.

The naturalist John Muir first traveled into the southern Sierra in 1873, climbing its peaks and exploring its rugged landscape. Two years later, he traced the belt of giant sequoias south from the Mariposa Grove. Accompanied by a mule, he crossed the North and Marble forks of the Kaweah River and climbed into a "noble forest," which he named the Giant Forest. Here he spent several days, camped inside Hale Tharp's hollow log, studying the Big Trees. Accounts of Muir's trips, published in a San Francisco newspaper, helped publicize the wonders of the southern Sierra.

John Muir
Explorer and naturalist of the Sierra

Muir described vividly the threatened destruction of the fragile beauty of Kings Canyon. Pragmatically, he urged that the forests be protected to retain moisture in the soil so that there would be enough water for San Joaquin Valley farmers during the dry summer months. Fires set by sheep-herders and overgrazing by millions of sheep gave rise to alarm. Clarence King noted that the Kern Plateau, which had been covered with meadows and lush grass on an earlier visit, now appeared as a "gray sea of rolling granite ridges."

Significant efforts to preserve the southern Sierra began in 1878 when editorials in the *Visalia Delta* criticized logging of giant sequoias, including a few exceptionally large trees for exhibition in the east. Led by George W. Stewart, the young city editor, the newspaper called for a fine or imprisonment for cutting giant sequoias. Leading men of science in both the eastern United States and Europe also expressed alarm. Secretary of the Interior Carl Schurz recommended that the president be immediately granted the authority by Congress to set aside at least two townships (a township comprises thirty-six square miles) in both the coastal and the Sierra sequoia belts.

In 1880, Theodore Wagner, the United States Surveyor General for California, suspended four sections (a section is one square mile) of the Grant Grove from entry, temporarily prohibiting anyone from claiming the land under existing land laws. This action came too late to protect the entire grove, as Daniel M. Perry had already made a homestead entry for 160 acres—this property has remained in private hands ever since. The following year, a local group led by William Wallace, together with members of the Langely expedition, proposed a national park to include Mount Whitney and the upper Kern Canyon in the high Sierra. Fearing that logging interests would block legislation that incorporated valuable timberland, they excluded the pine, fir, and sequoia forests on the western slope from their park proposal.

In response to growing local interest in preserving the southern Sierra, Senator John F. Miller of California introduced a bill to establish a national park. The measure received little support and died in committee, perhaps because the idea of national parks had yet to gain widespread acceptance. Also, the vast size of the proposed reserve would have led to opposition by timber and livestock interests, and private property in the sequoia belt of the Kaweah River watershed would have posed a major obstacle to establishment of a park.

Private Lands and the Kaweah Colony

Land could pass into private ownership through several laws, including the Preemption Act, Homestead Act, Timber and Stone Act, and Swamp and Overflow Act. Under the Timber and Stone Act, a person could purchase a 160-acre tract of surveyed, nonmineral land whose value lay chiefly in its timber and stone. Although designed to provide settlers with building materials for their sole use and benefit, the act's wording allowed considerable fraud. Dummy buyers purchased timberland for $2.50 an acre after arranging to sell it for a small profit to another party.

The Swamp and Overflow Act also was misused, as surveyors fraudulently declared much of the land in and around the Giant Forest to be "swamp and overflow," thus making it available for purchase. Legally, over 50 percent of each division so designated had to be truly marshy land. In fact, much of it was boggy only in the spring when the snow melted, and dried out in the summer. The story goes that surveyors in the Giant Forest would declare an area swamp and overflow for a consideration of twenty-five cents an acre. In this way, it became property of the state of California and could pass into private hands.

The greatest controversy involving suspected fraud arose over the land claims of the Kaweah Colony. With the intent of founding a utopian community, more than fifty members of the Cooperative Land and Colonization Association filed ownership claims in 1885 on extensive tracts of land in Giant Forest under the Timber and Stone Act. The association asserted that not a single claim would be worth less than "Fifty Thousand Dollars at the lowest market rate," based on the value of standing timber. They next sought capital for a railroad to connect with a road they planned to build from the foothills to the forest lands. When the railroad plan failed, they formed a joint stock company, the Kaweah Cooperative Commonwealth Company, and constructed an eighteen-mile road through rugged country approximately five miles from the edge of Giant Forest—a remarkable accomplishment. After setting up a portable sawmill, the colonists produced a small amount of lumber.

The Kaweah Colony, between 50 and 300 residents at any given time, consisted in part of skilled trade union laborers. In the spirit of their socialist experiment, they named the most prominent giant sequoias after their heroes: the tree now known as the General Sherman was then called the "Karl Marx." Idealism prevailed, at least at first, including equal rights for women and education for all. In reality, the colonists encountered financial

The Advance Guard—Kaweah Colony Road in 1889

crises and internal unrest. Short on cash, they developed their own currency, which was based on time contributed in labor to community projects.

While a government land agent, suspicious of fraud, examined the Kaweah Company's land claims, the Commissioner of the General Land Office temporarily prevented acquisition of property within eighteen townships under existing land laws, thus blocking its transfer to the Kaweah Colonists or any other private parties. Some residents of Tulare County initiated a drive to protect the Sierra forests permanently through an act of Congress. Farmers wanted to protect the watershed on which they depended for irrigation, and a growing number of summer vacationers wanted to preserve the groves of giant sequoia as scenic and recreational areas.

George Stewart and the Campaign for a Park

George W. Stewart, editor of the Visalia *Delta*, spearheaded the movement that led ultimately to the establishment of Sequoia and General Grant National Parks and the Sierra Forest Reserve. A native Californian born near Placerville in 1857, Stewart came to Tulare County as a boy. He first visited the Sierra Nevada in 1875 and formed what became a lifelong bond with the mountains and the giant sequoias. The following year, he began writing for the *Delta* and helped instigate the park bill of Senator Miller, which failed in the early 1880s. After spending a few years working on newspapers else-

where, he returned to Visalia in 1885, joined two others to establish the Delta Publishing Company, and became editor of the *Delta*. In 1889, he was alarmed by both private and public attempts to acquire parts of the Grant Grove. Although the Grove had been withdrawn from the market in 1880, Congress had done nothing to guarantee its permanent protection. Stewart warned of the damage sheep and man-made fires could cause to the watershed and thus to the valley below.

The *Delta's* editorials soon attracted local attention, and members of the Tulare County Grange called for a meeting that took place in Visalia on October 9, 1889. Prominent citizens who attended from Fresno, Kern, and Tulare counties agreed unanimously to petition Congress to establish a national park. When Stewart and Tipton Lindsey, former receiver of the U.S. land office, drew a map of the proposed reservation, they included the entire western slope of the Sierra from the present Yosemite National Park in the north to the

George Stewart
Father of Sequoia National Park

southern end of the forest belt in Kern County. They wanted to protect all major rivers flowing from the mountains into the San Joaquin and Tulare valleys.

A few months later, Stewart and his local supporters, especially Frank Walker, became alarmed over rumors that the federal government was about to open the Garfield Grove—south of Giant Forest—to private land ownership under the Swamp and Overflow Act, Timber and Stone Act, and other statutes. Lumbermen coveted the timber and sheepmen desired access to mountain meadows. The *Delta* staff mobilized interested groups and influential people from coast to coast, warning of the danger to the giant sequoias. Lindsey notified Congressman William Vandever, who then introduced a bill for a national park in the township that included the Garfield Grove. The *Delta*'s well-organized campaign attracted the support of *Garden and Forest, Forest and Stream*, and other publications. The California Academy of Sciences, American Association for the Advancement of Science, and American Forestry Association also adopted resolutions favoring the park bill. Stewart then enlisted the aid of California's Governor Robert W. Waterman, who sent a strongly worded telegram to Secretary of the Interior John Noble.

Finally, Stewart and his supporters sent telegrams to key people in Washington, urging them to help push the Vandever bill through the Senate and have it signed by the president in time to commemorate the fortieth anniversary of California's admission to the Union. On September 9th, Stewart, Walker, and other leading park advocates were in San Francisco attending the anniversary ceremonies when word came that they had something much closer to their hearts to celebrate: the park bill had passed the Senate the day before without debate or amendment. Two weeks and two days later, on September 25, 1890, President Benjamin Harrison signed the bill. The enabling act provided that two townships plus four sections be withdrawn from settlement, occupancy, or sale, and that they be set apart as a public park or pleasure ground for the enjoyment of the people. Sequoia National Park became the nation's second national park, created eighteen years after Yellowstone.

Stewart's expertise in government land law and his levelheaded approach to issues led to his later appointment as Register of the U.S. Land Office in Visalia. Two years before his death in 1931, many friends and Park Service officers gathered in Visalia to give him the recognition he so richly deserved. They acclaimed him the founder of Sequoia National Park and announced that Mount George Stewart, a peak on the Great Western Divide, had been named in his honor.

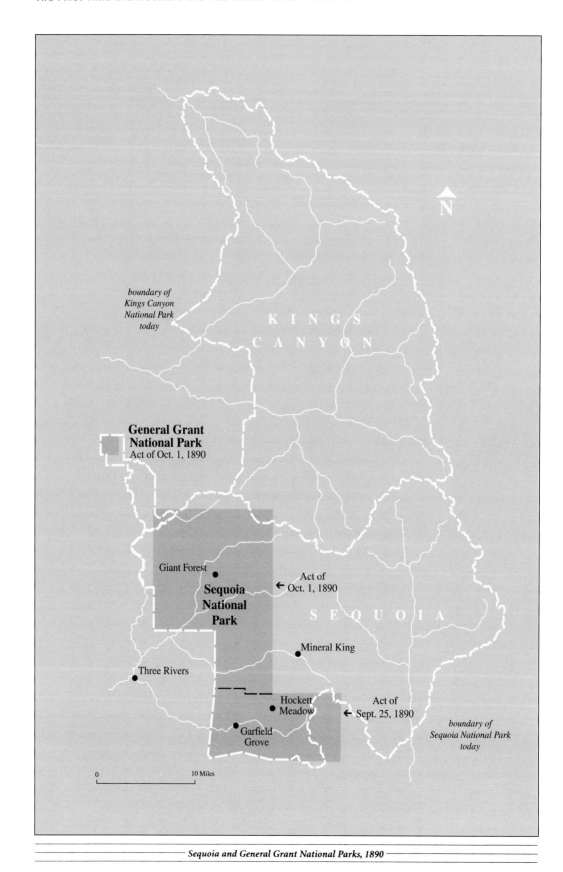

*boundary of
Kings Canyon
National Park
today*

K I N G S

C A N Y O N

**General Grant
National Park**
Act of Oct. 1, 1890

**Sequoia
National
Park**

Giant Forest

Act of
← Oct. 1, 1890

S E Q U O I A

Mineral King

Three Rivers

Hockett
Meadow

Act of
← Sept. 25, 1890

*boundary of
Sequoia National Park
today*

Garfield
Grove

0   10 Miles

Sequoia and General Grant National Parks, 1890

5 THE FIRST PARK ENLARGEMENT AND THE SIERRA FOREST RESERVE

ON OCTOBER FIRST, LESS THAN ONE WEEK AFTER THE CREATION of the park, Congress passed a second act. As originally introduced, the measure would have created a small Yosemite National Park. Shortly before Congress adjourned, however, Congressman Vandever sponsored substitute legislation that established a large Yosemite National Park, tripled the size of Sequoia, and set aside Grant Grove as a small separate national park. This legislation came as a complete surprise to Stewart and others who had worked so hard for the September twenty-fifth act.

While the origin of the October first legislation is uncertain, it seems probable that Daniel K. Zumwalt, a resident of Visalia, played a leading role. He visited Vandever in Washington and had a personal interest in protecting the Sierra watershed and in preserving the giant sequoias. More important, he was a land agent for the Southern Pacific Railroad, which had long been concerned about protecting the water supply of the San Joaquin Valley and which recognized that national parks would attract tourists and increase business.

The Southern Pacific Railroad, disliked and mistrusted in Tulare County because of its influence over state land-management policies, acted covertly to aid the park legislation. A map of the enlarged park on the railroad's stationery, dated October 10, 1890, is evidence that the Southern Pacific knew about the park enlargement at a time when no one else in California did. Contrary to custom, the substitute bill had not been printed, and it is possible that members of Congress who approved the bill did not realize that provisions enlarging Sequoia and preserving Grant Grove had been added at the last minute. It appears that support from the powerful Southern Pacific helped win the day for Sequoia, Yosemite, and General Grant National Parks.

Decline of the Kaweah Colony

Andrew Cauldwell, a special land agent of the Department of the Interior, reversed a previous report and ruled unfavorably on the colony's already-filed land claims in Giant Forest. He later had four trustees of the colony arrested for trespassing on government land and cutting government-owned trees. Despite widespread support of the colonists by many residents of

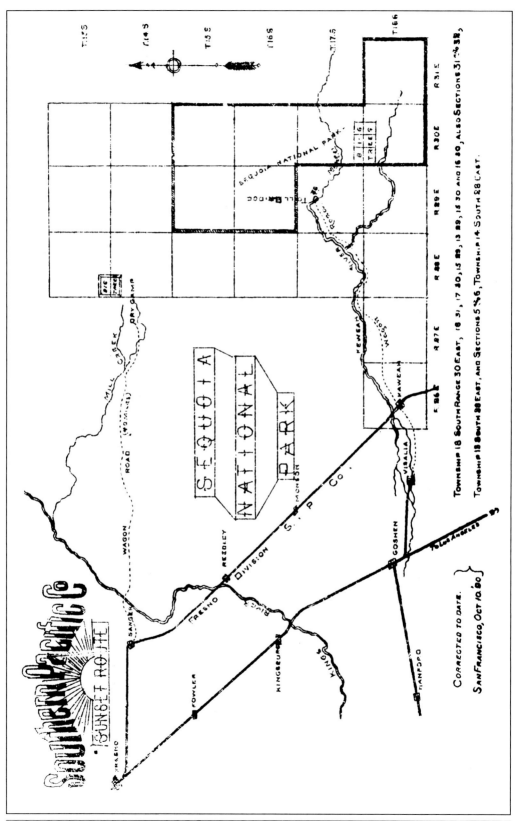

Southern Pacific Railroad map, October 10, 1890

Tulare County, who respected the time and labor that they had invested, in April 1891 Secretary of the Interior Noble decided against the colonists' land claims. A few days later, a federal court ruled against the trustees and levied a stiff fine.

Many of the colonists gave up and moved away. The remaining few leased 160 acres of privately owned timber land from the Atwell estate within the park and cut timber there. But the threat of legal action even brought this limited activity to a halt and the last hope of the Kaweah Colony withered away. Efforts to procure compensation from the government for the road they had built failed—technically, they had no right to the land they claimed. The government later completed the road to Giant Forest, the only access route for many years.

The Sierra Forest Reserve

The creation of the three national parks in California marked only the first step in protecting the Sierra Nevada. Further prompt action was clearly needed. During the 1880s, the population of Fresno and Tulare counties had more than doubled. The California State Board of Forestry frankly admitted that lack of funds prevented proper fire control. The American Forestry Association continued to call for protection of the Big Trees in Tulare County. Since most of California was still the property of the national government, the state looked to Washington for legislative help with land management.

Fortunately, in March 1891, Congress passed legislation that permitted the president to proclaim permanent forest reserves—today's national forests. Protectors of the Sierra could now propose that land be set aside in forest reserves or national parks; it mattered little that no clear distinction between the two kinds of reserves existed at that time. In April, Stewart recommended that Sequoia and General Grant National Parks be extended eastward to the summit of the Sierra Nevada. John Muir and Robert Underwood Johnson, editor of *Century Magazine*, both of whom had played a leading role in the establishment of Yosemite National Park, also continued to agitate for a large forest reserve in the southern Sierra.

In October, the commissioner of the General Land Office directed Special Agent B. F. Allen to investigate the forest reservation proposed in the Tulare County petition of 1889—a document that had only just arrived in the nation's capital. The petition requested that the government reserve a tract of land embracing over 200 townships. On Allen's recommendation, the commissioner withdrew 230 townships from settlement under federal land laws, pending investigation of these lands. While an "Anti-Park Association," led by local sheepmen and lumbermen, protested that the forest reservation would hurt local prosperity, most residents of the San Joaquin Valley either approved the withdrawal or were neutral about it.

Early in 1892, Johnson suggested to Secretary Noble that President Benjamin Harrison reserve all of the Sierra Nevada above a certain altitude. Johnson reasoned that Congress could convert some of it from forest reserve to park land at a later date—he dreamed of a large national park that incorporated the southern Sierra. Later that year, John Muir joined with twenty-six others in San Francisco to found the Sierra Club, an outing and conservation organization dedicated to the protection of the Sierra Nevada.

Special Agent Allen redrew the boundaries to exclude arable land in the foothills, thus eliminating a good deal of potential local opposition to the proposed reserve. When he completed his report in early 1893, he stressed the dependence of the economic future of the San Joaquin Valley on future tourism and the protection of the watershed. Finally, on February 14, President Harrison signed a proclamation establishing the Sierra Forest Reserve—a vast area of over four million acres stretching from Yosemite National Park in the north to a point well south of Sequoia National Park.

Cavalry troop assigned to guard the Parks, 1890s

6 EARLY PARK MANAGEMENT

CONGRESS IN 1890 PROVIDED NO INSTRUCTIONS OR FUNDING
for Sequoia National Park. At the request of Secretary of the Interior John
Noble, the Secretary of War sent troops to protect the national parks of
California from trespassers and vandals, a practice introduced earlier in
Yellowstone. But the troops lacked authorization to patrol the Sierra Forest
Reserve and there were not enough soldiers for this purpose anyway.

Protecting the parks proved difficult at first. When soldiers arrived in
June 1891 and made a camp outside the park at Mineral King, they found
many parts of Sequoia inaccessible even to patrols on horseback. J. H.
Dorst, Captain of the Fourth Cavalry and the first acting superintendent of
the park, complained that the High Sierra near Mount Whitney and the
Kings Canyon had been so overrun by sheep that he could find no grass for
his horses and pack animals. Hunters killed game, particularly deer, as
winter snows forced the animals from the high mountains. After October
first, when the troops withdrew for the winter, there was no way at all to
protect the animals, even within the park. Sheepherders persisted in driving
their sheep across the poorly marked park boundaries. Cattle also created
problems as local stockmen realized that the park superintendent had no
power to make arrests. The only penalty—expulsion from the park across
the nearest boundary—failed to deter trespassers from repeated illegal entry.

The gravity of the situation came home to Captain James Parker, acting
park superintendent, when he investigated the high Sierra country in June
1894. To make the arduous trip, he counted on feed for his pack animals
along the way. But the sheep had all but destroyed the once-lush meadows,
and when Parker posted a hundred notices warning trespassers to stay off
the newly created forest reserve, the sheepherders promptly tore them down.

In the absence of adequate sanctions for rule infractions, the troops
devised their own penalties. They drove trespassing cattle and sheep far to
the north, into the rugged Kings River country, while expelling herders
across another, far-distant boundary. The herds were found again, if they
were found at all, only after great expenditure of time and effort. This
practice ended cattle trespass, but sheepherders continued to risk entry into
remote areas of the park.

In 1898, acting superintendent Lieutenant Henry B. Clark pondered the
purpose of a national park: "Is it a playground for the people, a resort for

——————— *Acting Park Superintendent Charles Young (first row center without a hat), the only Black commissioned* ———————
——————— *officer in the U.S. Army, and his crew celebrate completion of the road to Giant Forest, 1903* ———————

the tourist, a mecca for travelers, a summer house where the inhabitants of crowded cities can repair and fill their lungs with the pure air of mountain and forest?" If so, he concluded, Sequoia was a failure, for its scenic wonders remained inaccessible.

Two local ranchers, John Broder and Ralph Hopping, echoed Clark's complaints when they opened a stage line between Visalia and their homes on the North Fork of the Kaweah River. They operated pack trains into the park and opened "Camp Sierra" in the Giant Forest. Clark, Broder, Hopping, and others urged construction of a road to the giant sequoias. In response, in 1900, Congress authorized $10,000 for the protection and improvement of the park. These funds allowed for repair of the old Kaweah Colony road and its extension into Giant Forest. Completed in 1903, the Colony Mill Road opened the door at last to those who wished to visit Giant Forest. Annual appropriations by Congress allowed for ongoing improvements in roads and trails in Sequoia and General Grant, and the trickle of tourists grew slowly but inevitably into a steady stream.

Private capital also had an impact on the parks. In 1898, the Mount

Whitney Power Company began constructing a series of hydroelectric power plants on branches of the Kaweah River. Local farmers welcomed such development, as it would provide energy to pump water for irrigation. Since national parks lacked a clear mandate and had no strong protector in the nation's capital, the Department of the Interior bowed to local business pressure and granted permission for the company to construct roads, flumes, and dams within Sequoia National Park. Only failure by engineers to locate bedrock at Wolverton prevented construction of a dam at this site. Even so, a power plant straddled the park boundary and new roads and flumes intruded into the park itself.

In spite of the valuable service provided by the military guard, the continued use of troops had its drawbacks. Temporarily assigned troops could neither know the parks well nor take the same interest in their protection as would park rangers. The almost annual rotation of acting army superintendents, each with his own interests and ideas, made continuity of management policy all but impossible. Captain Dorst called for protection of endangered species in the Sierra, for instance, while Captain E. S. Wright reflected the opinion of many later acting park superintendents when he called for organized hunts to eliminate "harmful animals" such as mountain lions. Military troops gradually gave way to civilian rangers. These rangers were first employed sporadically in Sequoia and General Grant

Walter Fry
First civilian Park Superintendent

during the Spanish-American War and then steadily after 1900. Park ranger Ernest Britten provided the first winter protection, beginning in 1900, and Walter Fry assumed the position of superintendent of the two parks in 1914. By that year, the military had withdrawn permanently, and Fry supervised a small staff of permanent and seasonal rangers. He inherited parks that had changed little since their establishment in 1890. They were still little known and almost wholly undeveloped. Lack of a consistent policy by the military superintendents and by the Department of the Interior continued to cause confusion about how the parks should be managed.

First automobile to enter Park, 1906

Early park visitors at the General Sherman Tree

7 CREATION OF THE NATIONAL PARK SERVICE

WHILE PARK ADVOCATES HAD HOPED THAT THE KINGS and Kern watersheds—part of the Sierra Forest Reserve might soon be added to Sequoia and General Grant National Parks, in 1905 all forest reserves were placed under the jurisdiction of the Department of Agriculture. Congress soon changed their names to "national forests," and President Theodore Roosevelt designated part of the former Sierra Forest Reserve as the Sequoia National Forest. Under the Forest Service's utilitarian policy, the national forests remained open to many uses, including grazing, mining, and logging.

National park advocates, led by the Sierra Club, responded with a proposal that several small national monuments be established in the Kings River Canyon and in other nearby scenic areas administered by the Forest Service. Under the Antiquities Act of 1906, the president could protect land for its prehistoric, historic, scientific, or natural features. Robert B. Marshall, Chief Geographer of the United States Geological Survey, preferred a large park incorporating the Kings and Kern river watersheds rather than small enclaves of national monuments. In 1911, California Senator Frank Flint introduced a bill to create a vast national park in the southern Sierra. Advocates argued that an enlarged Sierra park would increase government appropriations, attract tourists, and stimulate the local economy.

These proposals encountered opposition from the Forest Service and many private economic interests that preferred that the Forest Service continue to manage this land. Stockmen, who paid only a small fee for grazing on national forest lands, would be excluded from national park lands. Hunters opposed the elimination of such a large hunting area. Prospectors claimed that much valuable ore would be excluded from use, and lumber interests decried the loss of valuable timber. Others argued that the natural features of the Sierra already had protection through their ruggedness and inaccessibility. Chief U.S. Forester Henry S. Graves requested that all proposals for new national parks be deferred until a bureau of national parks was created.

A champion of such a bureau appeared in Stephen T. Mather, a successful businessman and frequent visitor to the Sierra. On one such excursion he met John Muir, who urged him to oppose commercial encroachment by loggers, miners, and others. The basic problem was that thirteen national parks and eighteen national monuments in the United

Stephen Mather
First Director of the National Park Service

States lacked sufficient protection and funds for management and development. While visiting Sequoia and Yosemite National Parks in 1914, Mather observed cattle grazing in the parks, poor roads and trails, and private land inholdings in the most scenic areas. His irate letter of protest to Washington against such mismanagement proved well timed, for a campaign to establish a national park bureau had been gaining momentum. In January of the following year, Mather arrived in Washington to assume a new job—assistant to the Secretary of the Interior in charge of national parks.

Mather recognized that creation of a national park bureau depended on congressional support. One approach was to get congressmen into the parks. To this end, he led a group of twenty-five influential men on a pack trip from Giant Forest to the Kern Canyon and Mount Whitney country in the summer of 1915. Included were Frederick H. Gillett, ranking Republican on the House Appropriations Committee, Gilbert Grosvenor, editor of *National Geographic Magazine*, and Ernest O. McCormick, vice-president of the Southern Pacific Railroad. To keep everyone happy, Mather brought along a renowned Chinese cook, Ty Sing, and had fresh fruits and vegetables hauled into the mountains daily at his own expense.

Mather lobbied Washington relentlessly for a national park bureau, convinced that only a vigorous national park service could block devastating raids on the parks. The 1913 loss of Yosemite's Hetch Hetchy Valley to a dam site to provide water for San Francisco boded ill for the future. If Yosemite could be desecrated, Mather reasoned, would any national park be safe? Hard work by preservationists finally paid off. Mather heard the good news in 1916: Congress had authorized the National Park Service.

8 PARK ENLARGEMENT

THE CREATION OF THE NATIONAL PARK SERVICE did not silence those opposed to expanding Sequoia National Park. The very size of the proposed enlargement, more than five times the 1890 park acreage, spurred antipark activists. Cattlemen in the San Joaquin Valley still coveted summer grazing lands in the mountains; cabin owners in Mineral King Valley worried about future use of their properties; the Forest Service argued that any future park would exclude timber, mineral, and grazing lands of commercial value; the Los Angeles Bureau of Power and Light promoted major dams at Cedar Grove in Kings Canyon and Tehipite Valley. Its rival, the San Joaquin Light and Power Company, filed applications for its own water storage and power sites, and local irrigationists defended their need for the water and hydroelectric power of the Kings River.

The contest between rival interests ended in a standoff and left the door open for negotiations. The Federal Power

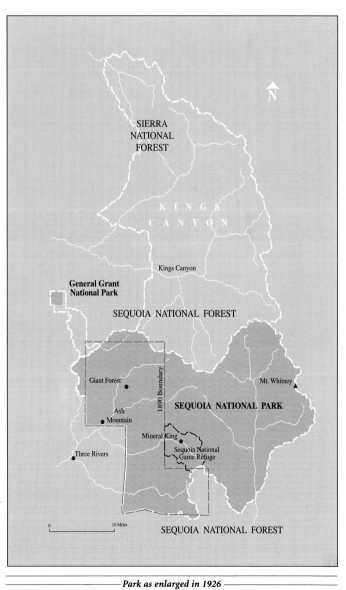

SIERRA
NATIONAL
FOREST

KINGS CANYON

Kings Canyon

General Grant
National Park

SEQUOIA NATIONAL FOREST

Giant Forest

1890 Boundary

Mt. Whitney

Ash
Mountain

SEQUOIA NATIONAL PARK

Mineral King

Three Rivers

Sequoia National
Game Refuge

0   10 Miles

SEQUOIA NATIONAL FOREST

Park as enlarged in 1926

Commission decided that Los Angeles had no immediate need for hydroelectric power from the Kings River and that the city's claims conflicted with the proposed park expansion. The irrigationists, however, succeeded in excluding the whole Kings Canyon watershed from the proposed park expansion, claiming that they would need sites for future hydroelectric power projects. In addition, the Park Service excluded the Mineral King Valley, believing the area to be too compromised by disputed land titles, prior mining activity, and summer cabins.

Mather and the Sierra Club, which had played a central role in the negotiations, decided to settle for what they could get—the magnificent Kern Canyon and the Sierra Nevada around Mount Whitney—and to work for a power-free Kings River park later. Mineral King remained under Forest Service administration as "Sequoia National Game Refuge." Three southern townships coveted by the Forest Service, including Hockett Meadow and the Garfield Grove, were retained by the park.

These compromises helped silence opposition to park enlargement. Government appropriations and tourist spending encouraged many to support park expansion as good business. With almost all opposition at least temporarily silenced, the bill had a clear road through Congress and received President Calvin Coolidge's signature on July 3, 1926.

Mount Whitney

9 CREATION OF KINGS CANYON NATIONAL PARK

DISCUSSIONS ON PROPOSALS TO ADD THE KINGS CANYON REGION to the national park system continued through the late 1920s. Once more, park advocates and irrigation and hydroelectric power interests could not agree on whether the area should be preserved for its scenic and recreational value or for the construction of dams. Developers rejoiced in 1930 when the Federal Power Commission issued a report listing nineteen potential dam sites in the Kings River watershed, including many high-alpine basins. It soon became apparent, however, that the report rested on a cursory field trip and included unreliable cost estimates. Discredited, the report carried little weight.

Meanwhile, the Forest Service considered various options, including an enormous tourist development in Kings Canyon, one with six hotels, camping for 6,000 people, a trans-Sierra highway, and an airstrip. At the same time, the Forest Service, in cooperation with the State of California, began constructing a thirty-mile road from General Grant National Park to Cedar Grove. After completion of the road, four campgrounds opened in Kings Canyon to serve the anticipated increase in tourists. Uncertainty over proposals for dams, plus the ongoing quest for a national park, forestalled further development. Perhaps to appease preservationists, the Forest Service also proposed a "primitive area" in the higher mountains of the South and Middle forks of the Kings River.

The battle over Kings Canyon accelerated in 1935 when the outspoken and influential interior secretary, Harold Ickes proposed a bill to establish Kings Canyon National Park. Ickes announced that the new park would be treated as "primitive wilderness," a land use classification in its infancy. This meant that the land in the park would be kept in its natural state, accessible only on foot or horseback except for the state highway to Cedar Grove then under construction. Many business interests in the San Joaquin Valley sharply criticized Ickes' proposal, and local Forest Service leaders fought to defend their control and management of land against what they regarded as an empire-building National Park Service.

The Park Service countered with a spirited campaign of its own. While downplaying its bureaucratic rivalry with the popular Forest Service, Park Service officials promoted a park via public speeches and radio addresses throughout the state. In valley towns, they argued that a park would

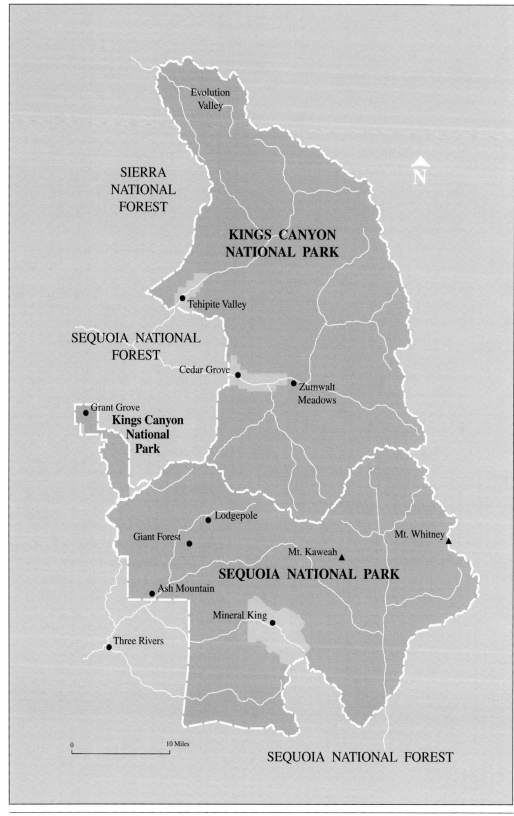

Evolution
Valley

SIERRA
NATIONAL
FOREST

N

KINGS CANYON
NATIONAL PARK

Tehipite Valley

SEQUOIA NATIONAL
FOREST

Cedar Grove

Zumwalt
Meadows

Grant Grove
Kings Canyon
National
Park

Lodgepole

Giant Forest

Mt. Whitney

Mt. Kaweah

SEQUOIA NATIONAL PARK

Ash Mountain

Mineral King

Three Rivers

0   10 Miles

SEQUOIA NATIONAL FOREST

Sequoia and Kings Canyon National Parks, 1940

stimulate tourism. They also allayed fears of valley business interests, assuring them that the Department of the Interior would look after their need for water. Since Ickes administered the Bureau of Reclamation as well as the National Park Service, these promises had the intended effect.

By 1939, a compromise began to emerge. To win the favor of the irrigationists, especially the powerful Kings River Water Association, Ickes and local Congressman Bertrand W. Gearhart supported legislation to develop the Pine Flat reservoir and other smaller reclamation development projects outside of the park. In addition, dam sites at Cedar Grove on the South Fork of the Kings River Canyon and Tehipite Valley on the Middle Fork were omitted from the park, leaving the door open for their future development. With these assurances, the irrigationists withdrew their opposition. Fortunately, the city of Los Angeles, its appetite for water temporarily satiated with the completion of the huge Boulder Dam on the Colorado River, no longer posed an obstacle to a park.

The compromise met with a mixed response from preservationists. The National Parks Association and the Wilderness Society opposed any park bill that excluded the beautiful floor of Kings Canyon and Tehipite Valley. In contrast, the Sierra Club thought that protection of the high Sierra far outweighed the omission of the two valleys on the western slope. The club argued that it would be wisest to establish a park now and work for the addition of contested areas, such as the floor of Kings Canyon and Tehipite Valley, at a later date. Ickes assured the club that a Kings Canyon park would be administered for its wilderness values and that the Park Service would keep development of recreational facilities to a minimum.

To everyone's surprise, a political scandal helped tip the balance in favor of the park. Congressman Alfred Elliott of Visalia, a rival of Gearhart and an opponent of the park bill, received a letter from a park advocate. Enclosed by error was a check for $100 to Gearhart, intended as a contribution to citizen groups supporting the park movement. Elliott seized the opportunity to attempt to entrap his political rival in a bribery scandal. He made copies of the check, alerted the FBI, and then sent the original check in a new envelope to Gearhart as if nothing had happened. He also made sure that local opinion leaders in the San Joaquin Valley received copies of the check. The entrapment scheme backfired, as Gearhart returned the check to the donor, suggesting that it be sent to the Sierra Club. On the floor of the House of Representatives, an angry Gearhart presented evidence of Elliott's mean-spiritedness. Elliott retreated in humiliation and Gearhart's park bill gained a sympathetic hearing.

In spite of last-ditch opposition by local Forest Service leaders, the California Chamber of Commerce, the Farm Bureau, and others—and in spite of the conflict among preservationists themselves—the park bill finally passed Congress. President Franklin D. Roosevelt signed the legislation on March 4, 1940, thus ending a fifty-nine year struggle to establish Kings Canyon National Park.

The new park was perhaps the best compromise possible at the time. The Park Service gained a magnificent mountain wilderness of more than

450,000 acres carved out of Sequoia and Sierra National Forests. The *New York Times* reported that the new park "consists of towering mountains, breath-taking canyons, sapphire-blue lakes and flowered alpine meadows in the gorges of the Kings River." Under the legislation, the Redwood Mountain Grove of giant sequoias near the General Grant Grove was soon added to the park. The small General Grant National Park, created in 1890 and administered jointly with Sequoia National Park for many years, was converted into part of the new Kings Canyon National Park. Since 1943, the neighboring parks of Sequoia and Kings Canyon have been administered jointly.

Backcountry wilderness, Kings Canyon National Park

10 PARK MANAGEMENT UNDER THE NATIONAL PARK SERVICE

ADMINISTRATION OF THE NATIONAL PARKS CHANGED MARKEDLY after creation of the National Park Service in 1916. With its small committed staff of professionals, the new agency became a permanent advocate for the parks. It set forth a well-intentioned but contradictory set of administrative guidelines that caused no end of difficulty for future park managers: "to conserve the scenery and the natural and historic objects and the wild life therein, and to provide for the enjoyment of the same in such manner and by such means as will leave them unimpaired for the enjoyment of future generations." How the parks were to be preserved unimpaired and enjoyed by the public at the same time remained to be seen.

Californians Stephen Mather and Horace Albright took the lead in the formation and early operation of the Park Service—Mather as the first director and Albright as second-in-command. They understood the growing problems of inadequate roads and visitor facilities at Sequoia and General Grant National Parks. Each summer, for example, hardy visitors on horseback or in stagecoaches struggled up the steep and narrow Colony Mill Road. After 1913, occasional automobiles, chugging up the same dusty road, frightened the horses. At Giant Forest, visitors found ramshackle camps with inadequate water and sewage systems.

Mather and Superintendent Fry inherited a problem of private land

Captain Charles Young
Acting Superintendent of
Sequoia National Park, 1903

inholdings on some of the very best park land, including extensive acreage in Giant Forest and important meadowlands. Development of these properties threatened to impair the beauty of the park and add immeasurably to management problems. For more than two decades, military superintendents had tried to buy 3,877 privately owned acres, scattered in many different plots, that had been acquired prior to creation of the park. Captain Charles Young, the only black commissioned officer in the U.S. Army, had managed to obtain an option to purchase most of these lands in 1903. He estimated that all claims could be purchased for no more than $73,000, an average of $19 per acre. This included 160 acres in General Grant National Park offered for sale for $1600. In spite of Young's efforts and the bargain prices, a frugal Congress repeatedly rejected requests for appropriations. At the same time, entrepreneurs proposed subdivisions and promoted logging on these properties. Fortunately, several landowners in Giant Forest supported the national parks and waited for the government to appropriate funds to buy their land.

To stir Congress to make an appropriation, Mather offered to match Congressional funding with private donations. In 1916, he managed to get an option to purchase a key 670-acre tract in Giant Forest for $70,000. Ironically, this was approximately the sum for which all the private lands could have been purchased in 1903. At this point, financial assistance came from an unexpected source: Congress. In unprecedented legislation, Congress appropriated $50,000, and Mather persuaded the National Geographic Society to donate the remaining $20,000. Immediate purchase of the heart of Giant Forest followed.

So far so good, but alas, most of the rest of the patented land, including other tracts in Giant Forest, remained in private hands. Time was an important factor. Already, the privately owned 160 acres in General Grant National Park had passed into the hands of Andrew D. Ferguson of Fresno. The new owner subdivided the first 40 acres into 292 lots and planned to sell them for $50 a piece. The Park Service could not meet his unrealistic price of $65,000, and to this day, the summer community of Wilsonia still exists at the Grant Grove.

In the next few years, diligent effort and generous donations paved the way for the purchase of most of the remaining privately owned lands. Only good luck had kept subdivisions like Wilsonia from developing in the heart of Giant Forest.

The Administration of Colonel John Roberts White

The campaign to acquire privately owned lands had been left in Mather's capable hands. The development of tourist and resource management policies, however, needed strong local leadership. Mather found such a person in Colonel John Roberts White. Recently returned from World War I, White had met Albright while job-hunting in Washington. In a mere eight months, he advanced from temporary ranger to assistant superintendent at Grand Canyon National Park, and in June 1920, he assumed the superintendency of Sequoia and General Grant. He would play a leading role at the two parks for the next quarter-century.

Like Mather and Albright, White believed the best way to preserve the parks was to make them popular with the public. This meant new roads and visitor centers, more trails, and advertising to explain park wonders. Construction of a new road began in 1922 to replace the inadequate Colony

Mill Road. The new route, via the Middle Fork of the Kaweah River, provided much better access for automobiles. Plans soon included a thirty-mile link between Sequoia and General Grant. The "Generals Highway" would allow visitors to drive into one park and out the other in the same day. Indeed, with great fanfare, it opened to Giant Forest in 1926, and nine years later connected both parks. Construction of axial roads to Crescent Meadow, Lodgepole, and Wolverton, plus a state highway to Cedar Grove, virtually completed the present road network of Sequoia and Kings Canyon.

Roads reached only the western fringes of the park and came nowhere close to the region added to the park in 1926: the upper Kern River Canyon and Mount Whitney country. Colonel White regarded access to this backcountry wilderness as essential to educating visitors about nature. A trail-building program received vigorous support from the Sierra

Col. John White

Club, whose members sought expanded opportunities to explore and enjoy the new alpine park land. In 1933 the Park Service completed the highly publicized John Muir Trail, from Yosemite to Mount Whitney. Begun as a state project in 1915, the trail linked Sequoia to its more famous northern neighbor. Colonel White took a great interest in a second project, known as the High Sierra Trail. This carefully designed route connected Giant Forest with Mount Whitney and provided easy access to the backcountry for hikers and people on horseback. By 1934, Sequoia's trail system, like its road system, was virtually complete.

As road and trail construction proceeded, Mather looked for ways to improve the concession services at Giant Forest and Grant Grove. He believed a single concessioner would provide the best service and be the most accountable. Fortunately, some small local operators in the parks declined to renew their options and, after one trial monopoly failed, Mather convinced an old business friend, Howard Hays, to take over the Sequoia and General Grant operations.

With Mather's promise to support development, Hays and his brother-in-law, George Mauger, began operations in 1926, just as the new road opened to Giant Forest. After moving the dining and retail facilities to the new road, Hays began replacing old, dilapidated cabins with new ones. Between 1926 and 1930, the concessioner built more than two hundred cabins and tent-tops at Camp Kaweah, Pinewood Auto Camp, and Giant Forest Lodge. Hays and Mauger also rebuilt cabins in Grant Grove, but stated that their primary interest would remain Giant Forest, where the chief tourist attractions and the greatest opportunities for profit were to be found.

Coping with Many Visitors

During the first decade and a half of Park Service administration, visitation to the two parks increased more than eightfold as tourists enjoyed the new road, hiked the new trails, and filled the new cabins. Mather and the Park Service sought ways to make park visits more meaningful. Radio addresses, newspaper articles, and public speeches by White and others helped. The most effective means, however, began with the inauguration of an "interpretation" program in Yosemite in 1920. Two years later, Walter Fry introduced the program at Sequoia with a series of now-familiar guided walks, campfire programs, and museum displays. This service proved so successful and dovetailed so nicely with White's ideas about visitor education that by 1931, he had manipulated his budget and the National Park Service's Washington office to successfully create a department of naturalists. The impact of the program can be gauged by its overwhelming popularity.

Interpreting the natural world became a Park Service trademark in the 1920s, but park management left much to be desired. In keeping with the prevailing misconceptions about wild animals, wildlife was handled on a good animal/bad animal basis, much as under the military superintendents. "Good animals" included deer—often made tame by visitor feeding—while bad animals included any that preyed upon good animals. Thus mountain lions, coyotes, and bobcats were systematically trapped or poisoned. Fire suppression became truly effective with the addition of new fire roads, specially trained crews, and regular funding. While well-intended, vigorous fire-fighting resulted in dangerous accumulations of flammable material. World War I had brought a return of cattle grazing to Sequoia, a wartime expediency that Mather and his new agency diplomatically allowed. It took until 1930 to remove the livestock—an early lesson to the Park Service that a policy once established, no matter how destructive, was hard to revoke.

Although most visitors thought the parks were well-run and fully protected, Colonel White and many of his staff began to doubt the efficacy of

some park management policies. The new construction and publicity had
succeeded in drawing unwieldy crowds. On July 4, 1930, more than 2,000
cars carrying some 4,300 people entered the park. White grimly recorded
the scene at Giant Forest, where a jostling, honking, mechanical jam spilled
out of the parking lots and alongside roads. Campsites overflowed onto
access roads and trash littered built-up areas. Visitors ran shouting through
the groves, scaled fences protecting the best-known sequoias, and engaged in
every form of amusement from softball to square dancing. Lost in the
disarray was the inspiration of the massive sequoias. White believed that
development for tourists had gone too far and that a park experience should
be more than fun and frolic.

As a result, Colonel White began to suggest new goals for park planning—goals of "atmosphere preservation" and visitor education. In order to
avoid the mistakes of the past, White declared himself an obstructionist,
ready to block or remove any policy or development that threatened the
parks' natural atmosphere. Additional impetus for this stand came from
professional landscape architects who advised White on almost every decision concerning park management. They supported preservation of the
natural scenery and urged that roads and buildings, if needed, blend into
their surroundings.

During the last two decades of his superintendency, White tried to mold
the parks according to his vision of natural preservation. Due to an unusual
set of circumstances, he achieved remarkable success. His seniority and
experience, coupled with eloquence and diplomacy, gave him an air of com-
mand rare in the Park Service. Further, the Great Depression placed a
powerful tool in his hands; White took charge of as many as 1,100 men in
the Civilian Conservation Corps, choosing projects within the parks and
allocating labor. Earlier in his career he might have built roads and buildings, opening thousands of acres to recreational development. Now he used
the CCC to maintain and replace existing facilities, to landscape large areas
of the visitor complexes, and to develop special attractions like Tunnel Log.
The CCC also increased White's influence indirectly. In administering a huge
CCC program nationwide, the Park Service developed a system of regional
offices and functional divisions that still exist. During the early days of this
expanded bureaucracy, the Park Service director and his Washington office
became more distant from local park decisions, thus creating a temporary
power vacuum into which Colonel White stepped.

Efforts to Control Development

A major battle to control park development began in 1927. Barely a year
after concessioner Howard Hays came to Sequoia, White suggested that he
abandon Giant Forest for a less environmentally sensitive pine-forested
valley at Lodgepole. Hays reacted with alarm. Citing visitor preoccupation

North Fork entrance, Giant Forest Road, 1920

Kenney Hotel, Round Meadow, Giant Forest, 1914

Giant Forest Museum, 1925

SEQUOIA NATIONAL PARK

At the Giant Forest there is a general store, telephone station, livery, and two photograph galleries.

The Kings River Parks Co. maintains a permanent public hotel camp in the Giant Forest. The authorized rates are as follows:

AUTHORIZED RATES AT GIANT FOREST CAMP

Board and lodging in camp without bath (American plan):

Per person, per day, two persons in room $4.00

Transient rates:

Breakfast 1.00

Lunch 1.25

Dinner 1.25

Lodging 1.50

Baths .... .50

Children 5 years and under, half rate.

Guests desiring extra tent room will be charged as follows:

Tent capacity of 4 persons occupied by two, per day each extra 1.50

Tent capacity of 2 persons occupied by 1, per day extra 1.50

Guest remaining at camps for a continuous period of one week or more, will be granted a reduction of 50 cents per day per person from date of first registration

Reprinted from 1921 National Park Service publication

Rules and Regulations, Sequoia and General Grant National Parks

Ranger Post Office at Giant Forest, 1910

with "sleeping beneath the Big Trees," he went over White's head to appeal to Mather. Like concessioners in many other national parks, Hays complained about the short tourist season, heavy maintenance expenses, and other hazards of doing business in regions remote from population centers. The first round in what became Sequoia's greatest management battle went to Hays and his company.

Although White acquiesced for a time, his consuming interest in restoring Giant Forest to its natural state led him to confront the concessioner again in 1931. Hays requested permission to add a few cabins to the accommodations complex known as Giant Forest Lodge. Recalling the distressing images of the previous Fourth of July, White rejected the application and again proposed that the company evacuate the grove. Hays again went over White's head with similar success. This time, however, the new Park Service director, Horace Albright, recognized the need for some restrictions on construction. He established a so-called "pillow limit," a maximum number of overnight guests, for the Lodge area. Park planners later identified this decision as the first limit of its kind in any national park. Pillow limits on other Giant Forest complexes soon followed.

In spite of Hays' victories, White successfully blocked other new developments. He defeated a proposal for another road from Ash Mountain to Giant Forest via the Middle Fork of the Kaweah River. More important, he helped defeat a proposal for a widely promoted high-altitude highway to run the length of the Sierra Nevada. He also blocked installation of electric power lines in Giant Forest

The Civilian Conservation Corps at work in Sequoia National Park

and rejected a variety of other proposals, ranging from golf courses and dance halls to hayrides and cable cars. Citing potential damage to the "atmosphere" of the parks, White repeatedly portrayed prodevelopment forces as tawdry and greedy.

Despite pillow limits, the problem of crowding in Giant Forest continued to concern park planners. White and his assistants explored various strategies for restoring the grove's inspiring atmosphere. They limited the amount of time campers could stay at the four government campgrounds. They encouraged winter use, hoping to distribute visitors seasonally. Instead, this strategy merely added to the swelling numbers. When they encouraged the concessioner to add improvements to Kings Canyon and Grant Grove to attract visitors away from Giant Forest, the offer was spurned as unprofitable. Park planners moved some government buildings to the Lodgepole area, but they were too few to make much of a difference. They even pondered redesigning the road system to decrease auto traffic. Nothing promised any real hope except full removal of concession facilities from the grove.

As a new decade dawned, White maneuvered to gain even tighter control over park planning and the concessions. The onset of World War II halted nearly all development and resource management programs. Visitation dropped by 80 percent, the parks' budget suffered a drastic cut, and the ranks of Park Service and concession employees declined sharply. Yet during the war years, planning for future development accelerated. Hays and Mauger hoped to replace some of the older Giant Forest cabins after the war and to expand the visitor complex. Colonel White hoped for a return to CCC-type labor for repair of roads and trails neglected during the war. He also hoped a combination of luck and strategically applied pressure would enable him to remove concession facilities from Giant Forest. In order to strengthen his position, White called on his traditional allies, landscape architects. Every one of them recommended removal of the concessions.

White's control over local development decisions weakened after the war, when the Washington office took back the reins. The imminent expiration of the concessioner's contract in 1946 intensified direct negotiations between Hays and the national office. Feeling powerless, White railed against the concessioner, the policy of lengthy contracts for monopoly concessions, and what he regarded as usurpation of his duties. When Hays' contract was temporarily extended, the Colonel bitterly predicted that the concessioner would stall by obtaining indefinite contract extensions until a more amenable Park Service administration took over.

By 1947, White's acrimony proved a stumbling block in the negotiations and resulted in his forced retirement. One of the most powerful superintendents in the system was replaced by Eivind Scoyen, whose attitude toward development was more lenient. A few years later, Park Service Director Newton Drury and Regional Director Owen Tomlinson also retired, to be replaced by people less committed to restoring Giant Forest to its natural state. Finally, in 1952, Hays and Director Conrad Wirth signed a new contract that ignored the question of Giant Forest. The era of John Roberts White, of local control, and of atmosphere preservation had ended. The problems White had recognized remained.

Traffic congestion in Giant Forest Village, 1953

Crowded Giant Forest campgrounds included increasing numbers of house trailers in the 1950s

The 'Bear Pit'   Sequoia Nat'l. Park

———— The Park Service discontinued the popular but misguided practice of feeding garbage to bears in 1940 ————

11 LATER ADDITIONS TO THE PARKS

THE CREATION OF KINGS CANYON NATIONAL PARK IN 1940
left many management questions unanswered. The most pressing were: who
should administer the small area suitable for tourist facilities at the end of the
road on the South Fork of the Kings River, and what sort of development
should be allowed? The Forest Service agreed to Park Service management of
the Cedar Grove area of Kings Canyon, even though the area remained under
the jurisdiction of the Forest Service. Financial considerations and continuity
of policy within the nearby national park influenced this choice.

The question of development proved more controversial. The Fresno
Chamber of Commerce argued for substantial improvements, while the Sierra
Club wanted the least amount of construction necessary to meet visitor needs.
Years passed without a decision, partly because neither the concessioner nor
the Park Service was willing to make a substantial investment in an area whose
future was uncertain.

In 1948, the City of Los Angeles made new proposals for water and power
development, not only within Kings Canyon and Tehipite Valley, but within the
park itself. Although Cedar Grove and Tehipite Valley together embraced
relatively few acres, they were important to the park. Cedar Grove represented
the one area in Kings Canyon that could be reached by automobile and be
developed for use by tourists; Tehipite Valley, dominated by a granite dome
that rose high above the Middle Fork of Kings River, provided an exceptional
geological attraction. Local irrigationists immediately refiled their own claims
and faced a second threat when the Bureau of Reclamation moved to develop
the North Fork of the Kings River as part of the massive Central Valley
Project. Local interests won on both fronts when the Federal Power Commission and the State Water Board ruled against Los Angeles.

When alternative dam sites, especially at Pine Flat, were identified
downriver, the irrigationists finally withdrew their opposition to including the
contested areas in the park. In 1965, Congress added Cedar Grove and Tehipite
Valley to Kings Canyon National Park. Construction of the long-awaited improvements at Cedar Grove, however, came only in the following decade after
electric lines reached the South Fork and a new concessioner, Government
Services, Inc., later renamed Guest Services, agreed to invest the needed capital.
By now, environmental awareness had spread and the Park Service approved
only a modest eighteen-room complex to serve the public.

Mineral King

Just as the decades-old battle over Kings Canyon ended, controversy broke out over Mineral King, south of Sequoia National Park. The former mining community, excluded from the park in 1890, had remained a quiet area for summer cabins and camping. The Forest Service administered the valley as part of Sequoia National Forest and, after 1926, as a game refuge. With the enlargement of the park that year, the valley became an enclave, surrounded on three sides by national park lands.

Responding to greater demand for outdoor recreation following World War II, the Forest Service invited proposals from private developers for a ski resort at Mineral King. Due to the high estimated cost, especially of the construction of an improved road, no acceptable developer could be found until the 1960s. Early in 1966, the Forest Service granted Walt Disney Productions a preliminary planning permit for a year-round resort. The Disney proposal included a Swiss-style village, ski-lifts to serve 20,000 skiers daily, and parking for 3,600 vehicles. In opposing the proposal, the Sierra Club argued that Mineral King's value as wilderness made the valley worthy of national park status and that, if developed, the valley would sustain irreversible damage.

At the end of the following year, Secretary of the Interior Stewart Udall bowed to mounting pressure and agreed to a proposal to construct an improved road across national park land into the valley. The Sierra Club responded, filing suit in 1969 in United States District Court for an injunction to block federal officials from issuing the necessary permits. Three years later, the United States Supreme Court upheld a ruling by the United States Court of Appeals that the club did not have the legal standing necessary to pursue the lawsuit. The Court, however, left the door open for the club to amend its original complaint in the District Court.

Faced with further delays and possible defeat in the courts, disappointed by the California legislature's refusal to fund improvements of the road to Mineral King, and aware of growing national public opposition to its plans, Disney looked elsewhere for a resort site. In 1978, Congress ended the controversy by adding Mineral King to Sequoia National Park as part of an Omnibus Parks Act—a landmark in preservation legislation.

12 THE RISE OF ECOLOGICAL MANAGEMENT

EARLIER, DURING WORLD WAR II AND ITS AFTERMATH, Congress had provided minimal financial support for the parks. While visitation to Sequoia and Kings Canyon increased nearly 125 percent between 1940 and 1955, funding increased at less than half that rate. As a result, the parks' infrastructure deteriorated, and park visitors encountered substandard facilities and crowded roads. Partly in an effort to garner public support for increased funding by Congress, the Park Service advocated a major ten-year development program—Mission 66. At the two southern Sierran parks, the project included two new visitor centers, extensive new employee housing, a new administrative center at Ash Mountain, and expansion of park infrastructure. Some in the Park Service feared Mission 66 would damage the parks and wondered what would save the "preservation" side of the Park Service's charter.

The application of ecological principles to park management provided a partial answer. Pioneering wildlife biologists Aldo Leopold and Joseph Grinnell helped shape future policy through their writings and the influence of many of their students who served in the Park Service. In the southern Sierra, forest pathologist Emilio Meinecke contributed a 1926 study of human impact on Giant Forest. Between the 1930s and 1960s, research scientist Lowell Sumner experimented with a deer reduction program, discontinued the Bear Hill show (a bizarre tourist attraction with bleachers surrounding a bear-infested garbage dump), institutionalized predator protection, and encouraged studies of backcountry meadows. Meanwhile, a burst of research activity in the late 1940s and early 1950s produced several extensive reviews of backcountry resources in the high Sierra.

In 1959, ecologist Richard Hartesveldt released the first of several studies on giant sequoias, challenging policies that allowed construction and suppressed fires among the Big Trees. In questioning fire suppression, Hartesveldt struck at the oldest and most dearly held directives of the earlier preservation policy. He argued that older trees were endangered by abnormal accumulation of fuel around the base of their trunks, and pointed out that sequoia seeds rarely germinated in areas choked with vegetation. Periodic fires would clear the debris, solving both problems.

During the 1960s, as the environmental movement caught hold, the philosophy of ecosystem management came to the fore. In 1963, a committee

of scientists commissioned by Secretary of the Interior Stewart Udall released a path-breaking report named after its chairman, A. Starker Leopold,
and ordered that it be implemented as the major policy guide for all parks.
It recommended that the Park Service "recognize the enormous complexity
of ecologic communities and the diversity of management procedures re-
quired to preserve them." It called for maintaining or recreating conditions
that "prevailed when the area was first visited by the white man." Such a

policy called for
personnel trained
in the biological
sciences. Later
studies reinforced
the report. Ecolo-
gist F. Fraser
Darling and geog-
rapher Noel D.
Eichhorn, for
example, stated
that the central
administrative
principle of park
management
should be "to
consider first the
ecological health

———— Meadow erosion along a heavily used trail ————

of a park so that it shall endure for posterity."

Faced with a groundswell of public and scientific support for wilderness preservation, Congress passed the Wilderness Act in 1964. This
measure designated more than nine million acres of national forest land as
the nucleus of national wilderness and provided that other federal lands be
considered later for possible inclusion in the system. Eventually, Congress
formally designated 85 percent of Sequoia and Kings Canyon National Parks
as wilderness.

Congress passed the National Environmental Policy Act in 1969, requir-
ing federal agencies to prepare statements on the environmental effects of all
major federal projects and to propose alternative plans to mitigate damage.
Preservation groups, whose membership grew rapidly because of the environmental movement, became the loudest and most persistent participants in
public planning.

At Sequoia and Kings Canyon, the impact of these changes first affected
the backcountry, the major area of the two parks. The 1961 publication of a
*Backcountry Management Plan for Sequoia and Kings Canyon National
Parks* followed reports on meadow ecology, a massive litter cleanup, and

tighter controls on hikers and large parties dependent on livestock. The plan became a blueprint for all other backcountry parks in the system. In it, the Park Service called for some meadows to be closed to stock use, the monitoring of trails and meadows, litter cleanup programs, and better organization of research projects. As the 1960s progressed, park planners closed more meadows to recreational stock parties and even, in some cases, to backpackers.

While the environmental movement led the Park Service to confront its problems of stock use, litter, and meadow damage, it also encouraged increasing numbers of backpackers to enter the backcountry. In the 1950s, researchers reported that Bullfrog Lake, high in southern Kings Canyon National Park, suffered from a shortage of firewood and forage as well as "hacked up trees, open can and bottle dumps, multiple criss-crossing trails, and all sorts of abandoned equipment and trash." Visitation to the Sequoia and Kings Canyon backcountry jumped from 8,000 in 1962 to more than 44,000 in 1971. A later study concluded that "a century of unregulated back country use has led to the development of over 7,700 dispersed undesignated campsites," and warned that recovery from human impact would be slow.

Armed with its ecological agenda and faced with the risk that people might love the delicate wilderness to death, the Park Service took a novel step. In 1972, in cooperation with the Forest Service, rangers began for the first time to issue wilderness permits that limited the number of people allowed into the most popular areas of the backcountry. That it did so on the basis of ecologically based principles was even more remarkable, given the Park Service's encouragement of backcountry use in earlier decades.

In addition, hikers in the backcountry learned a new set of rules: camp on bare ground at least 100 feet from streams and lakes (to protect vegetation and water quality); use established campsites where possible and avoid making campsite "improvements" (to minimize human impact); carry a lightweight gas stove (to avoid campfires and allow vegetation to decompose to nourish new plant life); avoid polluting the water (bury human waste and dispose of soaps or detergents far from water sources); and carry out all trash. Changed behavior, based on reeducation of the public, resulted in reduced impact on the wilderness. After 1975, when more than 48,000 people entered the backcountry, visitation stabilized and then began to decline as the baby-boom generation grew older.

In the 1970s and 1980s, an increasingly environmentally aware public advocated limited development within the parks, including the recently added lands at Cedar Grove and Mineral King. Only in Grant Grove did the public approve a plan for significant enlargement of tourist facilities. But even here, where the need was evident, the public advocated dispersal of the proposed buildings to minimize their size and impact on the environment.

Meanwhile, the Leopold Report continued to have a profound impact. Park scientists at Sequoia and Kings Canyon attempted to correct past mistakes with programs to eliminate exotics, reestablish native species such as golden trout and bighorn sheep, and separate bears from campers and their food. The most startling change came in fire management. In 1964 Hartesveldt began experimenting with prescribed burns in sequoia groves. The successful regeneration of giant sequoias that resulted from these experiments encouraged the Park Service to establish a permanent policy of controlled burning and monitoring of natural fires. By 1969, the program was fully underway in Sequoia and Kings Canyon and has since gained widespread public acceptance.

Of all management issues, development at Giant Forest remained the most difficult. In response to a report by a blue-ribbon Park Service panel, the government moved campgrounds, picnic areas, and most of its structures out of the area by 1972. However, the concessioner's more than 350 buildings remained scattered throughout the forest. In 1980, the Park Service released its *Giant Forest Development Concept Plan,* under which all commercial services in the grove would be eliminated and new overnight services would be constructed to the north at Wuksachi Village. Planners called for restoration of the Giant Forest to its natural state where possible. They envisaged park visitors enjoying the grandeur of the giant sequoias on quiet footpaths.

The late 1990s saw long-awaited changes in the Giant Forest area. At the end of the 1996 season, the historic Giant Forest Lodge complex near Round Meadow closed for the last time. By the end of 1998, all commercial facilities within the grove were permanently closed. At the same time, a new park concessioner, Delaware North Parks Services, undertook the construction of a new lodge complex away from the Big Trees area at Wuksachi Village near Lodgepole. Finally, the dreams of John White and others who early saw the mistake of over-developing the Giant Forest were coming to fruition.

13 QUESTIONS FOR THE FUTURE

IN THE LATTER STAGES OF THE TWENTIETH CENTURY, the Park Service recognized new problems. In an important report, *State of the Parks 1980*, the service noted that most threats to the national parks originated outside of park boundaries, For example, air pollution from the San Francisco Bay Area and the San Joaquin Valley drifted into Sequoia and

Kings Canyon National Parks. Visibility declined noticeably, ozone pollution threatened sequoia seedlings, and acid rain posed a risk to the alpine zone. How could the Park Service cope with such problems?

Sierra Club outing in Sequoia National Park, 1902

Park visitation had mushroomed over the decades. Sequoia received more than 1,000 visitors in 1908, 100,000 in 1927, and one million in 1950. By the 1970's the combined visitation to Sequoia and Kings Canyon surpassed two million. To protect the parks, the Park Service adopted new strategies, including a quota system for the backcountry and a reduction in facilities in heavily impacted tourist areas accessible by automobile.

In the 1980s and 1990s, the Park Service continued to struggle with its original mandate: to provide for recreation while protecting the parks unimpaired for future generations. At Mineral King, a congressional commitment to renew permits for summer cabins allowed continuation of recreational use incompatible with the preservation philosophy of the national parks. In the backcountry, stock use associations successfully defeated a plan that would have drastically reduced their access. The whole philosophy of ecosystem management continues to be rigorously scrutinized. No one can say what twist of circumstances might again be a reminder that parks are human creations, set aside by human design, and controlled by human ideas.

CONCLUSION

PUBLIC CONCERN FOR PARK PRESERVATION has advanced remarkably since the latter part of the nineteenth century when Congress created Sequoia National Park. At that time, most people looked at the land as a source of wealth from mining, logging, grazing, hydroelectric power generation, and other profitable ventures. Only a few people saw the value of protecting unspoiled scenic and recreational areas. By the second half of the twentieth century, times had changed. With greater affluence and more leisure time, Americans flocked to the national parks. Lands formerly prized for utilitarian purposes were now treasured for their natural environments. Americans had discovered belatedly that their wilderness heritage could be preserved only by public awareness and action.

The best hope for protection of these lands lies in adoption of the "land ethic" of Aldo Leopold. In *A Sand County Almanac*, Leopold states that all ethics rest upon a single premise: "that the individual is a member of a community of interdependent parts." His land ethic enlarges the boundaries of the community to include soils, waters, plants, and animals. Each individual must be responsible for the health of the land. "Health" he defines as the capacity of the land for self-renewal, and "conservation" as our effort to understand and preserve this capacity.

Leopold believes that the evolutionary process for a land ethic requires that people no longer consider land use solely on the basis of economic self-interest. "Examine each question," he says, "in terms of what is ethically and esthetically right, as well as what is economically expedient. A thing is right when it tends to preserve the integrity, stability, and beauty of the biotic community. It is wrong when it tends otherwise."

Environmental author Robert Cahn warns:

Conditions in the national parks provide an early warning signal that can alert the nation to what may be happening to the natural environment as a whole. They are also the nation's best indicator of what can be called its environmental ethic. They provide a measure of the willingness of today's citizens to adhere to a set of values that includes not only appreciation of the nation's natural and cultural heritage, but a desire to share it with others and leave it unharmed for future generations.

As the second century of Sequoia and Kings Canyon National Parks begins, ecological preservation seems well established as the operating management philosophy of the National Park Service. Yet it is just a philosophy, a set of current beliefs and practices. The future of Sequoia and Kings Canyon rests in the hands of the public and those who will manage park preservation in the century to come.

Early park naturalist program on Moro Rock

MAP CREDIT

Maps of Sequoia and Kings Canyon adapted from *Challenge of the Big Trees* by Larry M. Dilsaver and William C. Tweed, John Parsons, cartographer.

PHOTO CREDITS

Page 8 (top), page 40 and page 42 — Lindley Eddy, National Park Service.

Page 8 (bottom) — Detail from photograph, courtesy Department of Library Services, American Museum of Natural History.

Page 10 — Tulare County Historical Society

Page 15 — Bancroft Library

Page 30 — Mark Tilchen

Back cover — Dick Burns

Other photos are from the National Park Service collection.

INDEX